I0478900

MANDALAS
Adult Coloring Book

Volume 3

http://www.KipADoodles.com

ISBN: 1-886522-05-7
ISBN-13: 978-1-886522-05-3

Your Free Gift...

Want some free adult coloring pages? Want access to more freebies and special offers from Kip aDoodles?

As a way of saying thanks for your purchase of this coloring book, I'm offering **THREE FREE** adult coloring Mandala designs which are available only to my fellow color-ers! These pages are not sold anywhere else and can only be found via subscription.

Plus you will receive THREE NEW FREE adult coloring pages every month. And you will receive instant notification whenever I release a new coloring book, along with the chance to receive designs available *only* through my website. Finally, you will receive special discounts on all of my books!

Subscribe to my Email Newsletter and Download Your First FREE Pages Now!

Get the details here:

http://www.kipadoodles.com/subscribe

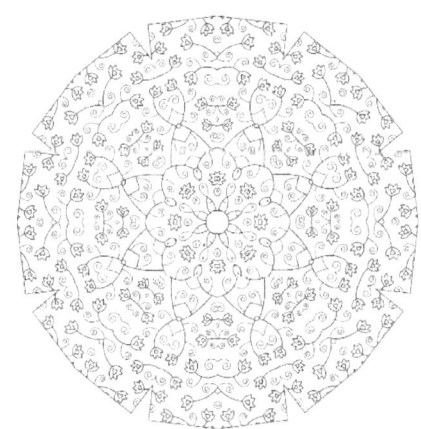 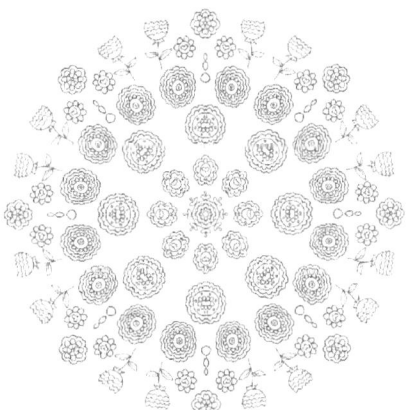 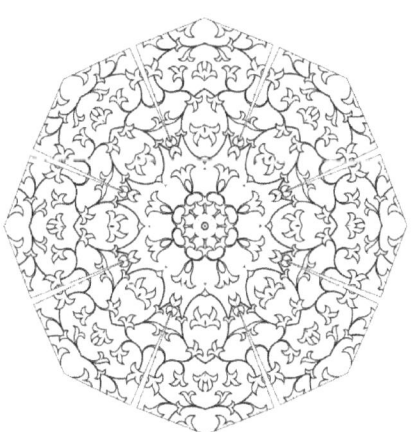

How To Enjoy This Book

Welcome to this Kip aDoodles coloring book!

    START ANYWHERE! Begin coloring on the page that captures your attention. If it's the first design, last design, or somewhere else in the book – that's the perfect place to begin your journey!

    TAKE YOUR TIME! There is no race, no competition, no schedule. There are no "right" or "wrong" ways to color these designs. You don't even have to stay within in the lines! The only rule is that you have fun!

    Coloring is a chance to release your inner child, to go back to those innocent days of youth. Coloring is also a great stress reliever! It is relaxing, meditative, and best of all, actual restful for your brain. In fact, by engaging the right side of your brain (the creative side), it can help your cognitive health!

    You'll have hours of fun, mindful calm and relaxation while you color the 25 original mandala designs in this coloring book. Each design is just waiting for you to bring it to life with color! Escape for a few minutes or hours at a time.

    The designs in this book range in complexity, but there is nothing too intricate for even a beginning colorist to enjoy. Printed on individual pages for easy coloring offers you two benefits: The coloring will not bleed through and ruin another picture. And your finished work of art can be removed and framed, if you want to.

    Easily color these designs with any dry media, like colored pencils or crayons. You can also color with gel pens or markers. If you decide to use gel pens, markers or another form of wet media, I recommend that you put an extra piece of paper or even poster board behind the design you're working on. This will ensure the wet media will not bleed through to other designs. With the more intricate designs, you might consider using ultra-fine pens or markers to easily color the smaller design areas.

Share the experience! Have you ever colored with your family or a friend? Or with a group? Discover the joy of sharing the phenomenon of coloring! Some communities even have coloring groups who regularly meet. What fun is that!

Please "Like" my Facebook page https://www.facebook.com/kipadoodles and share your completed artwork. Seeing how the designs come to life in your hands will be great fun!

IMPORTANT: *Please do not re-sell these images.* If you are interested in licensing my art or any type of commercial, educational or non-profit use, please email me at Kip@KipADoodles.com. I would love to hear from you!

After this book's coloring pages, you will find the **Coloring Companions Resources** list, with includes tools and coloring media to enhance your coloring experience.

And finally, at very end of this book is the link to my website and other popular coloring books. Be sure to check them out!

Any questions or suggestions? Don't hesitate to email me Kip@KipADoodles.com.

Happy coloring!

Kip@KipADoodles.com

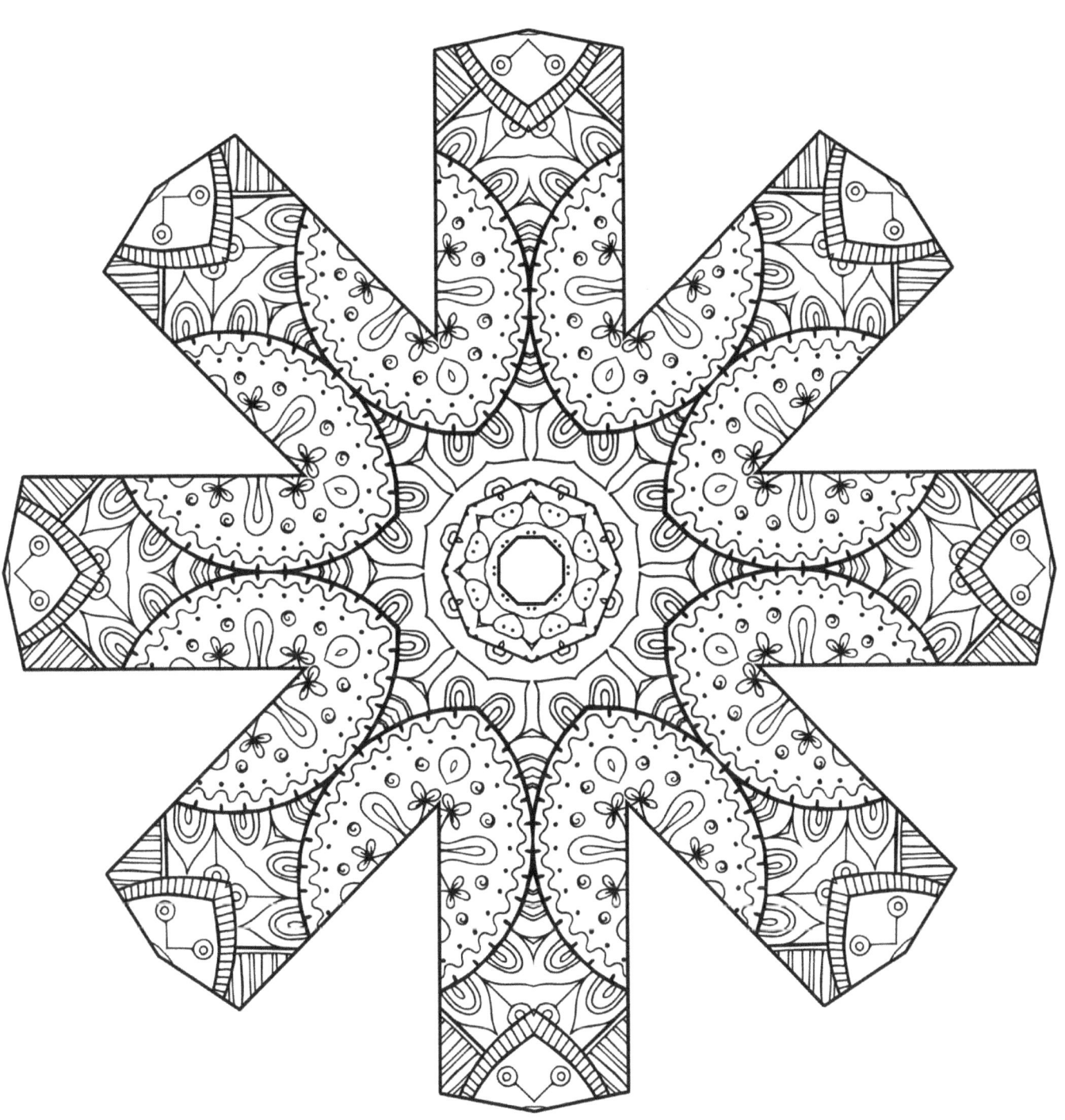

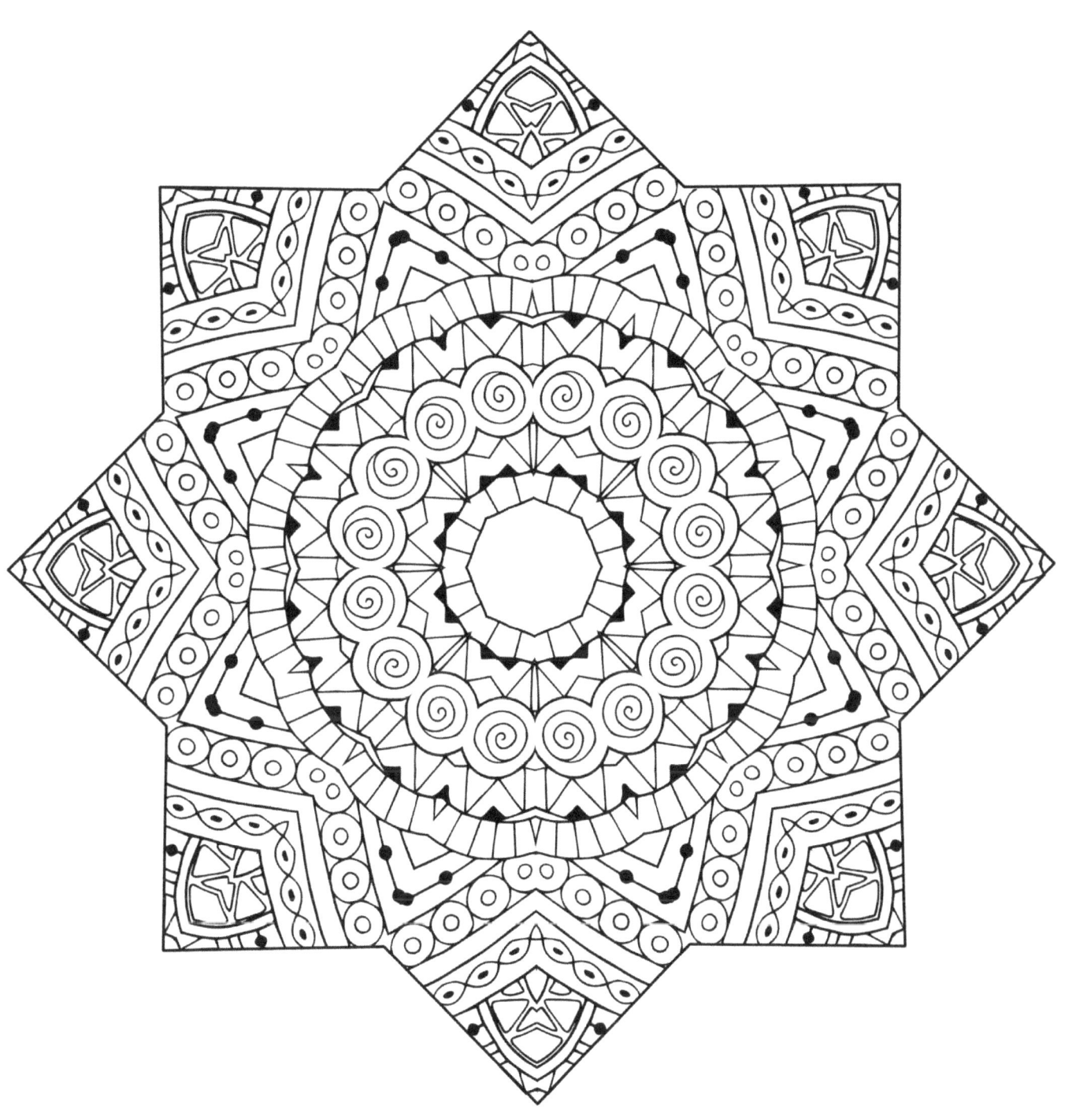

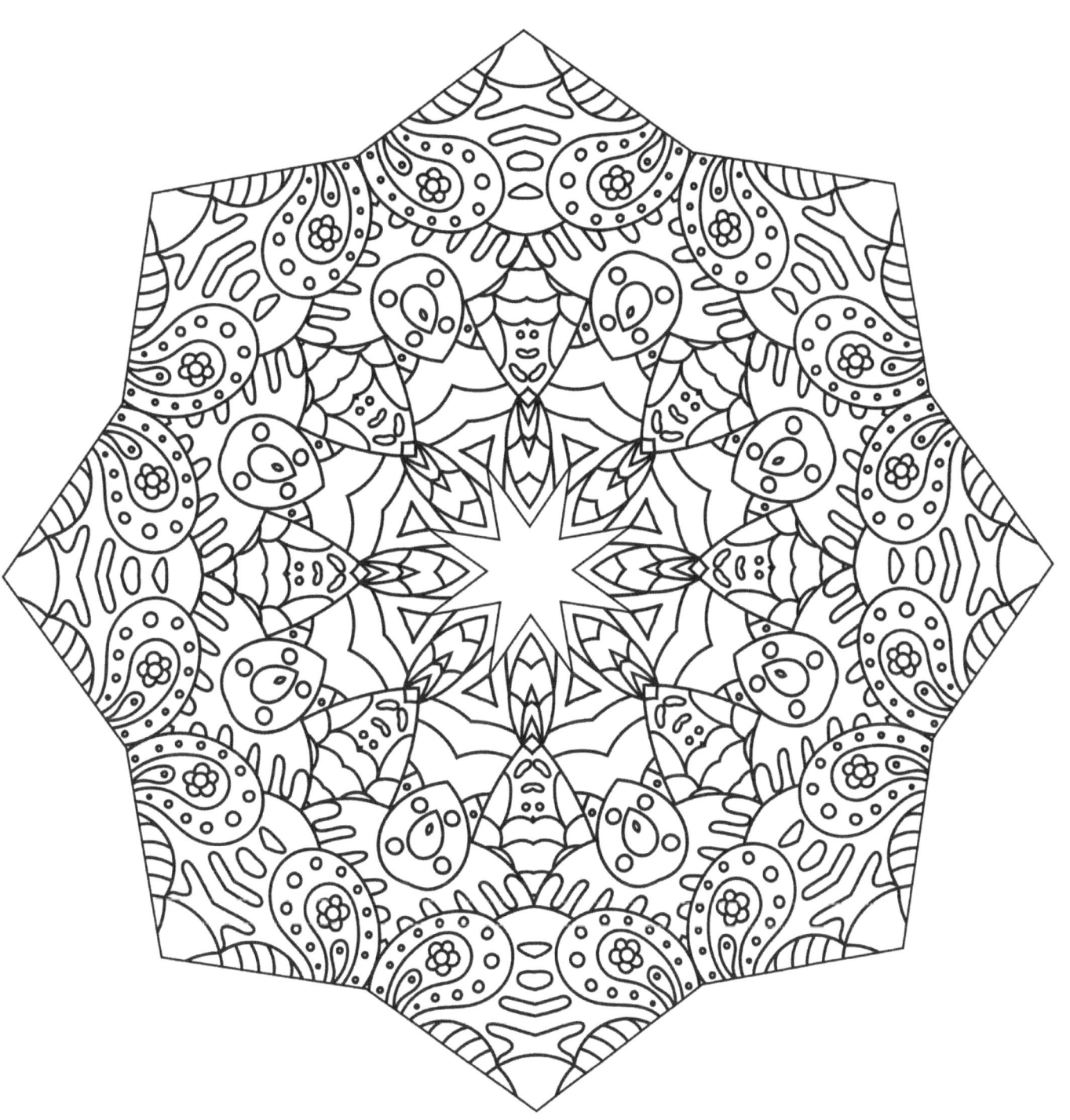

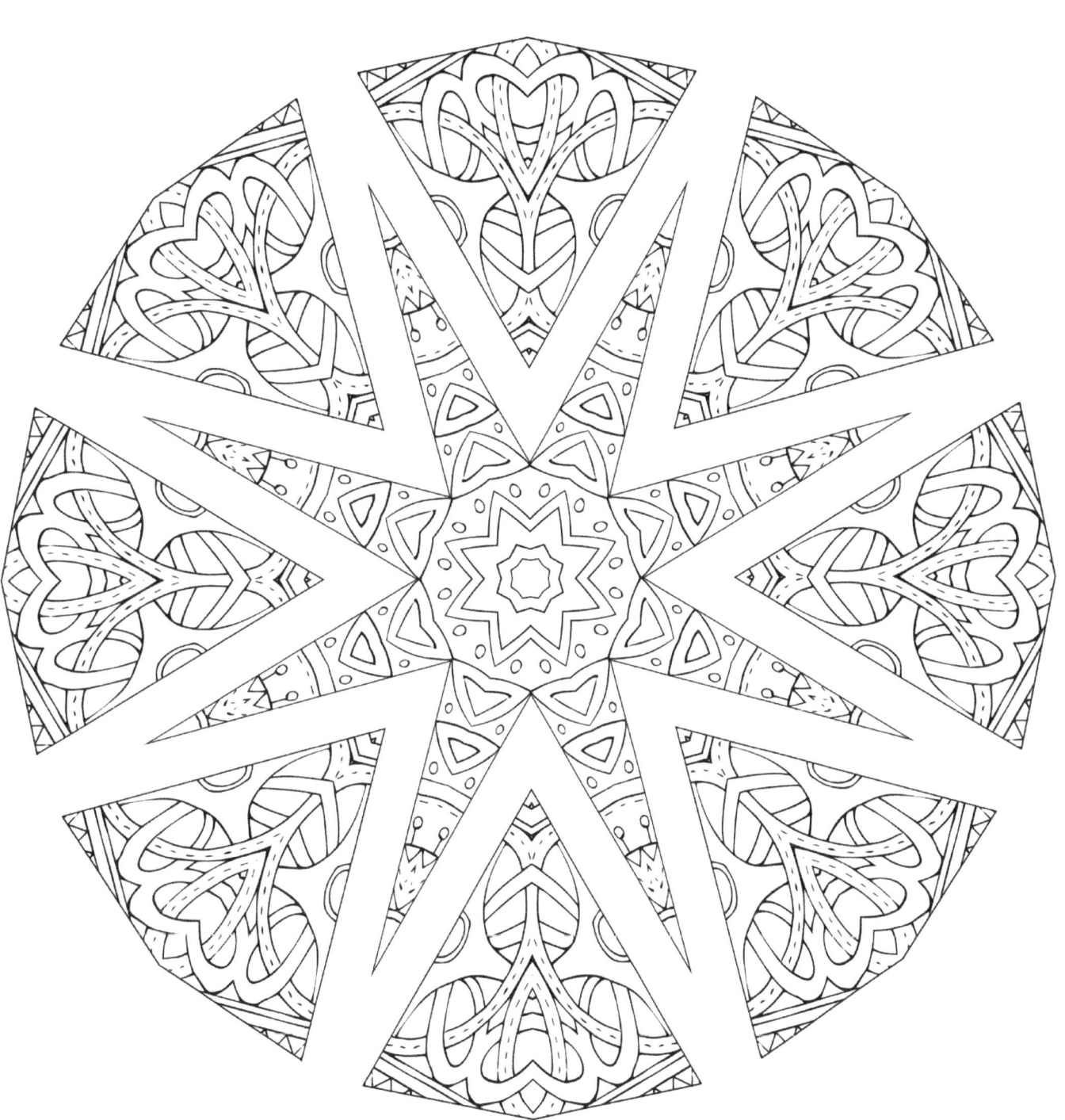

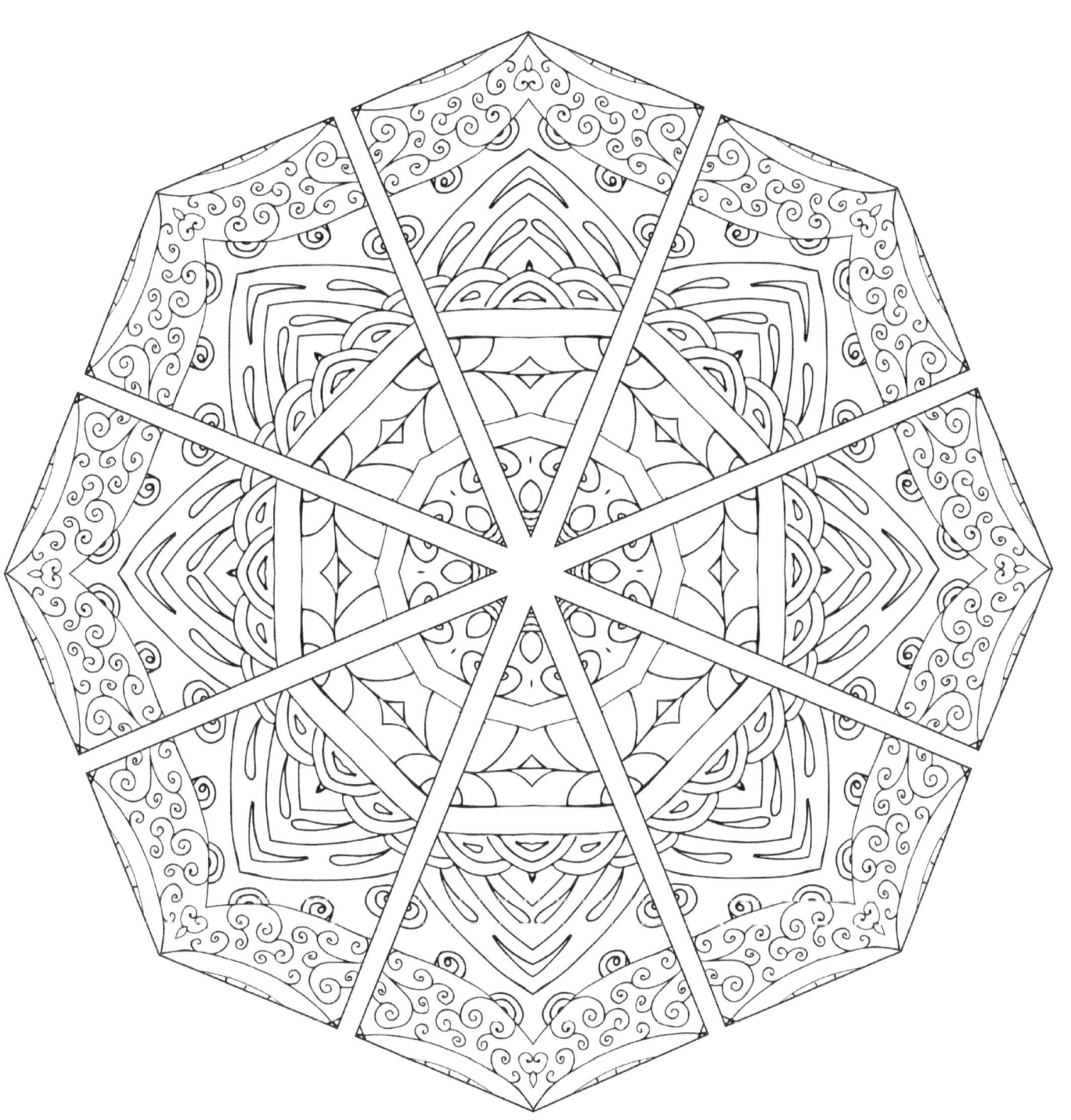

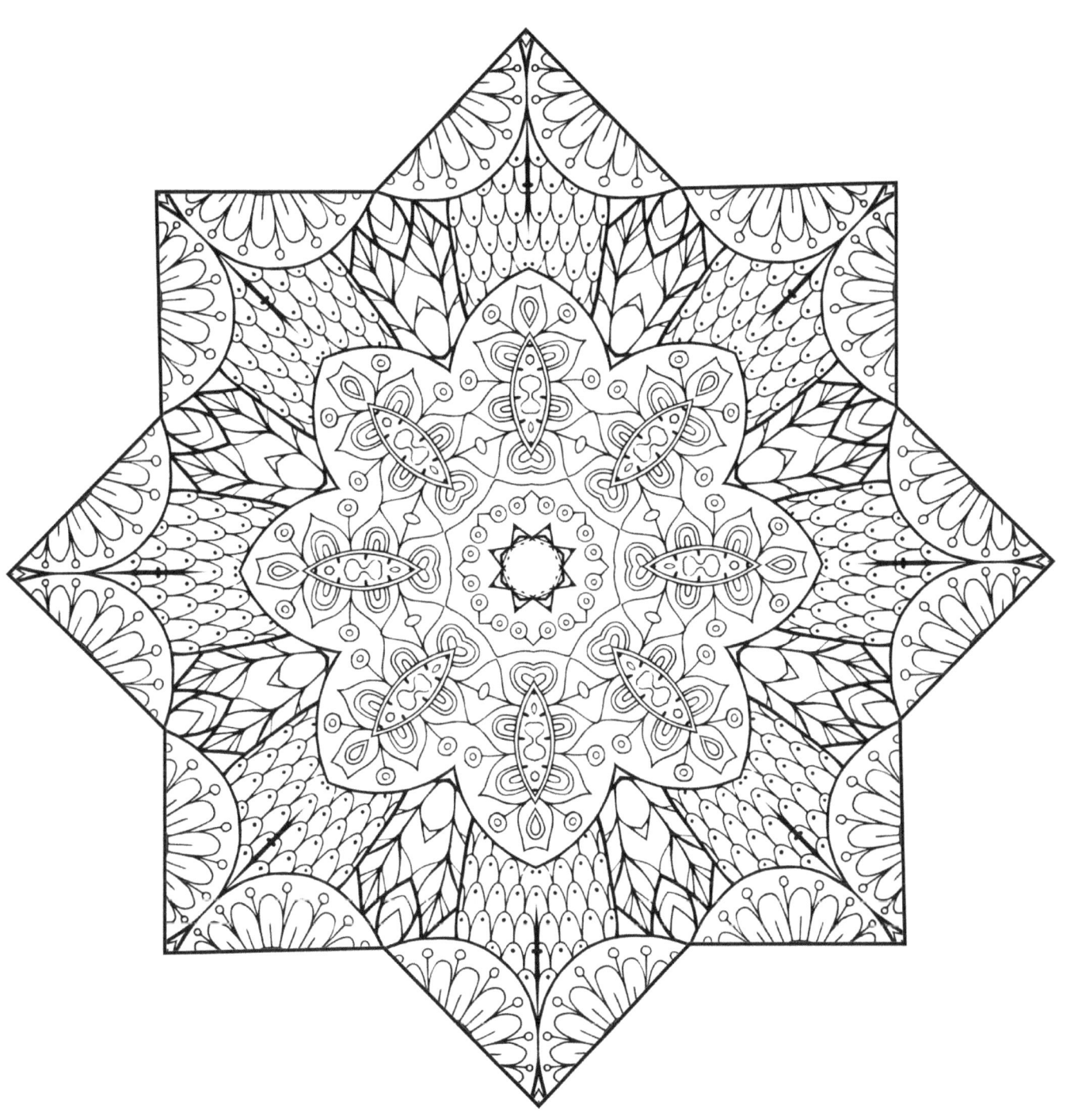

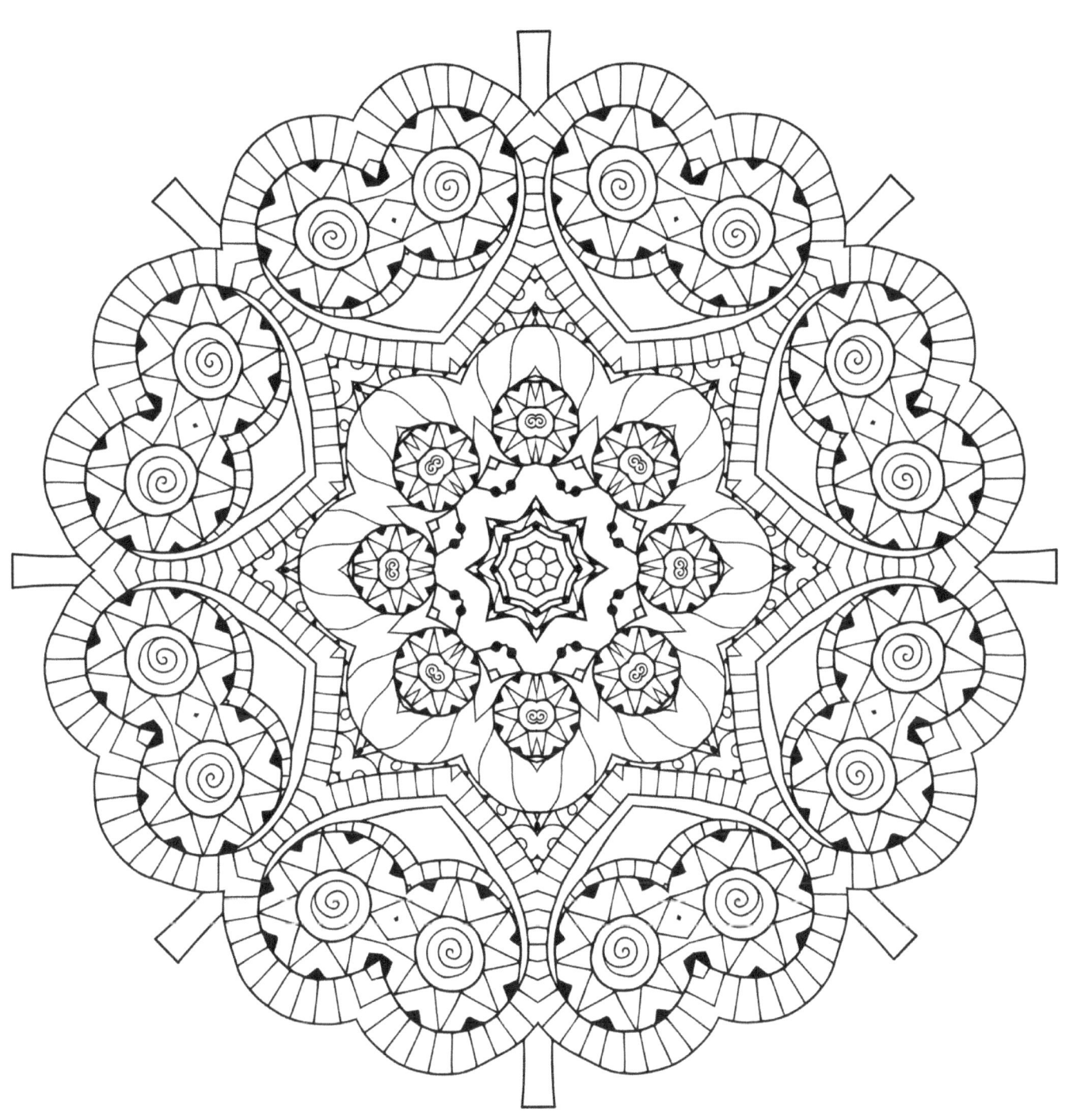

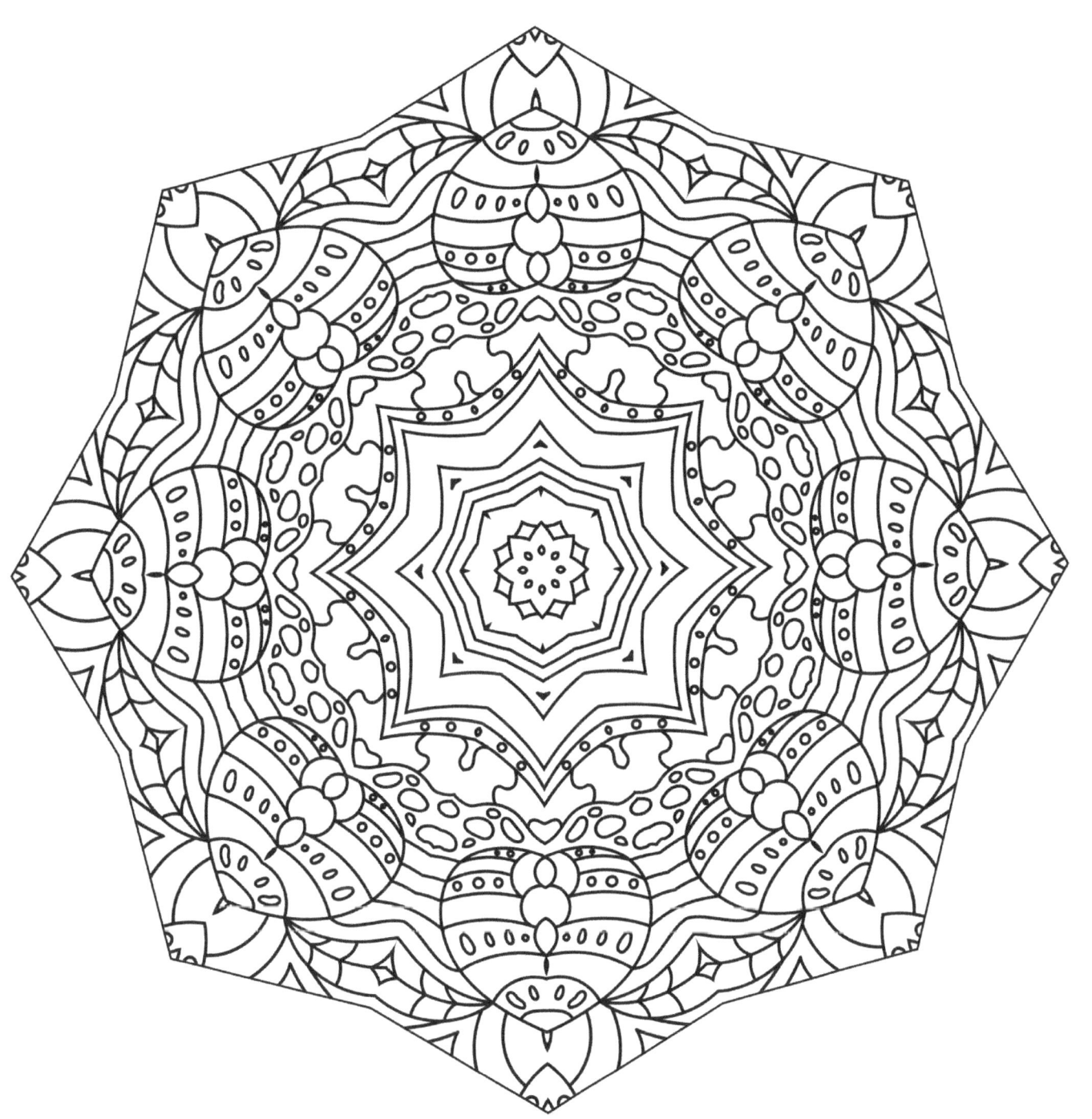

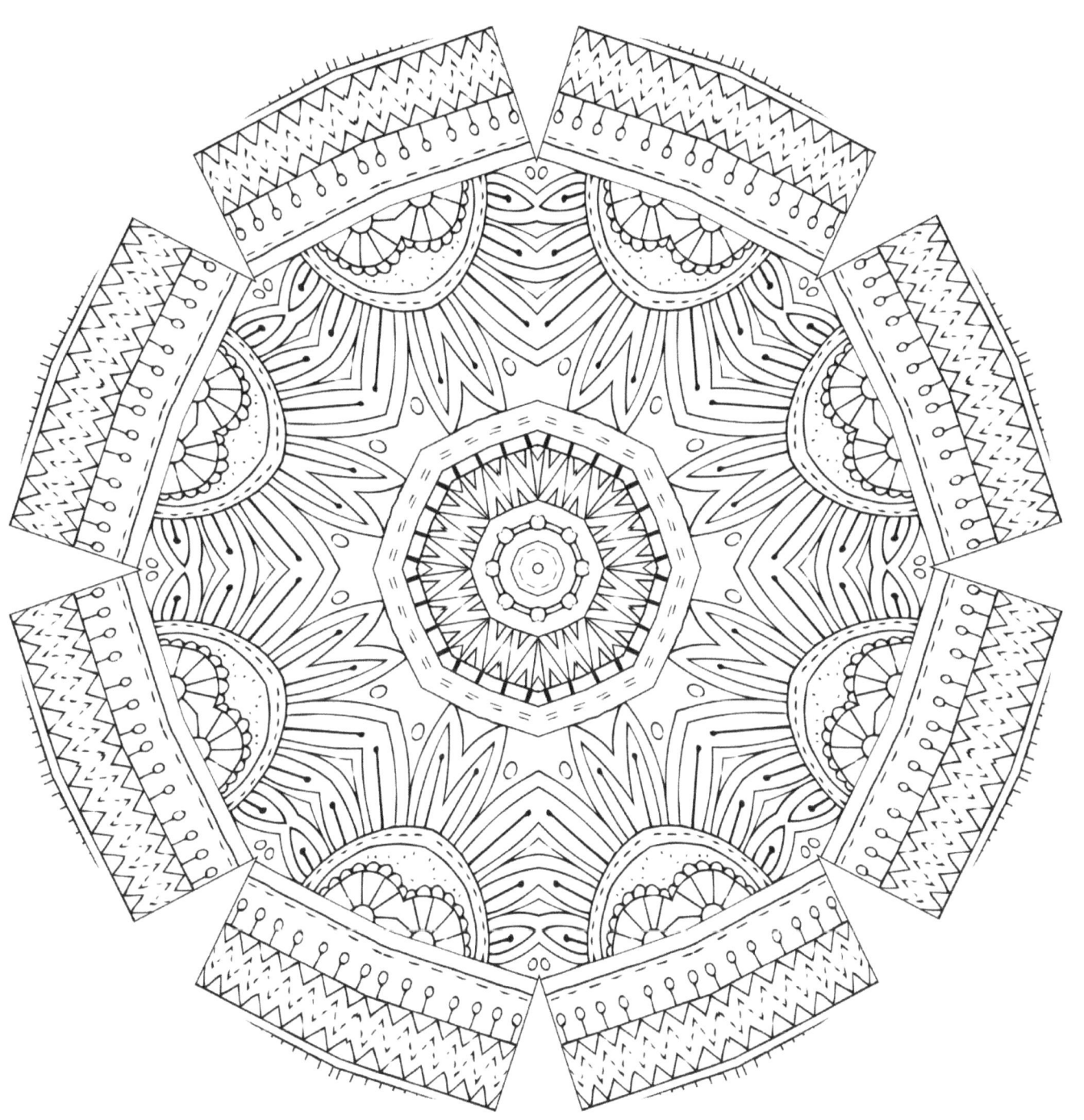

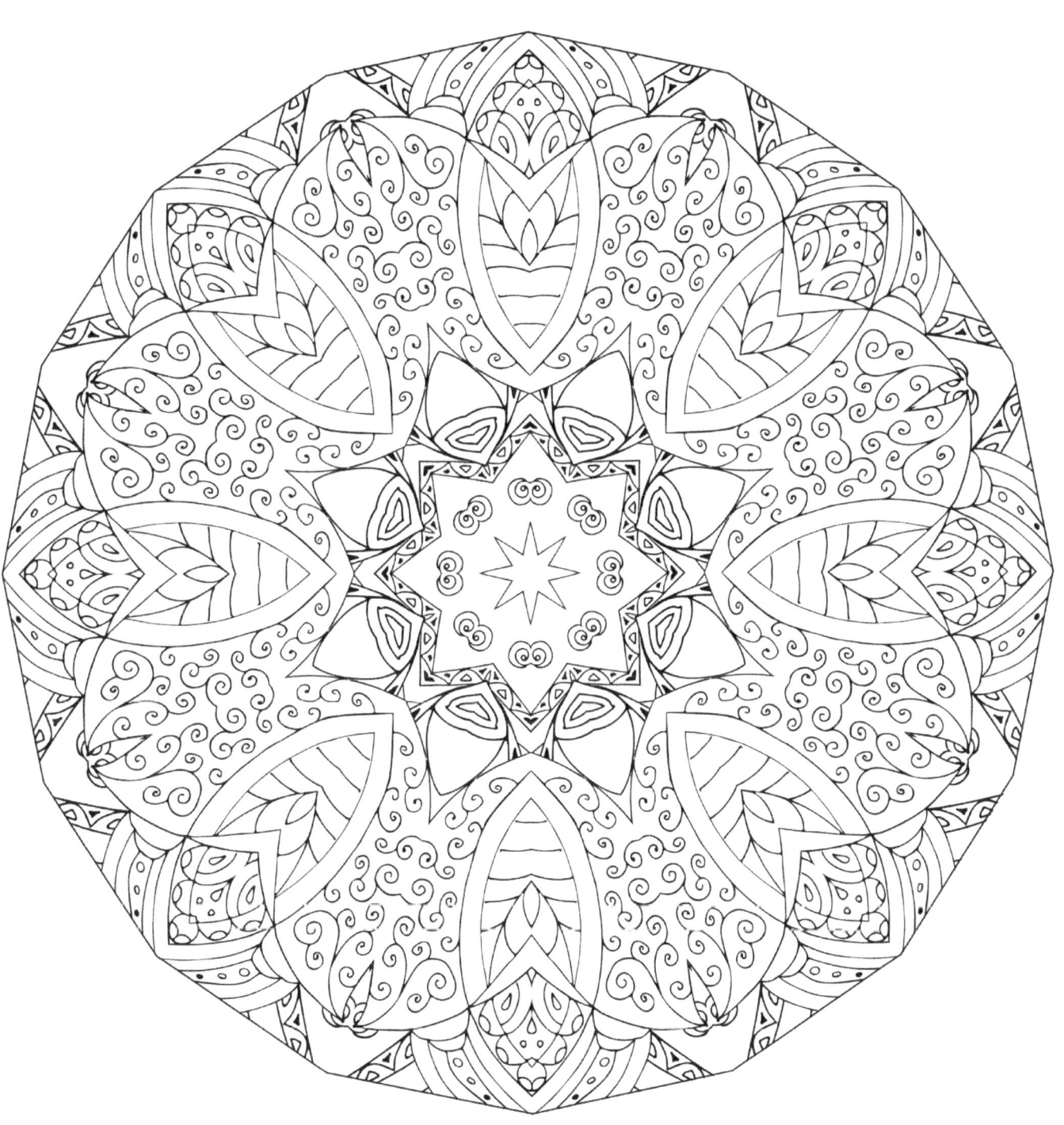

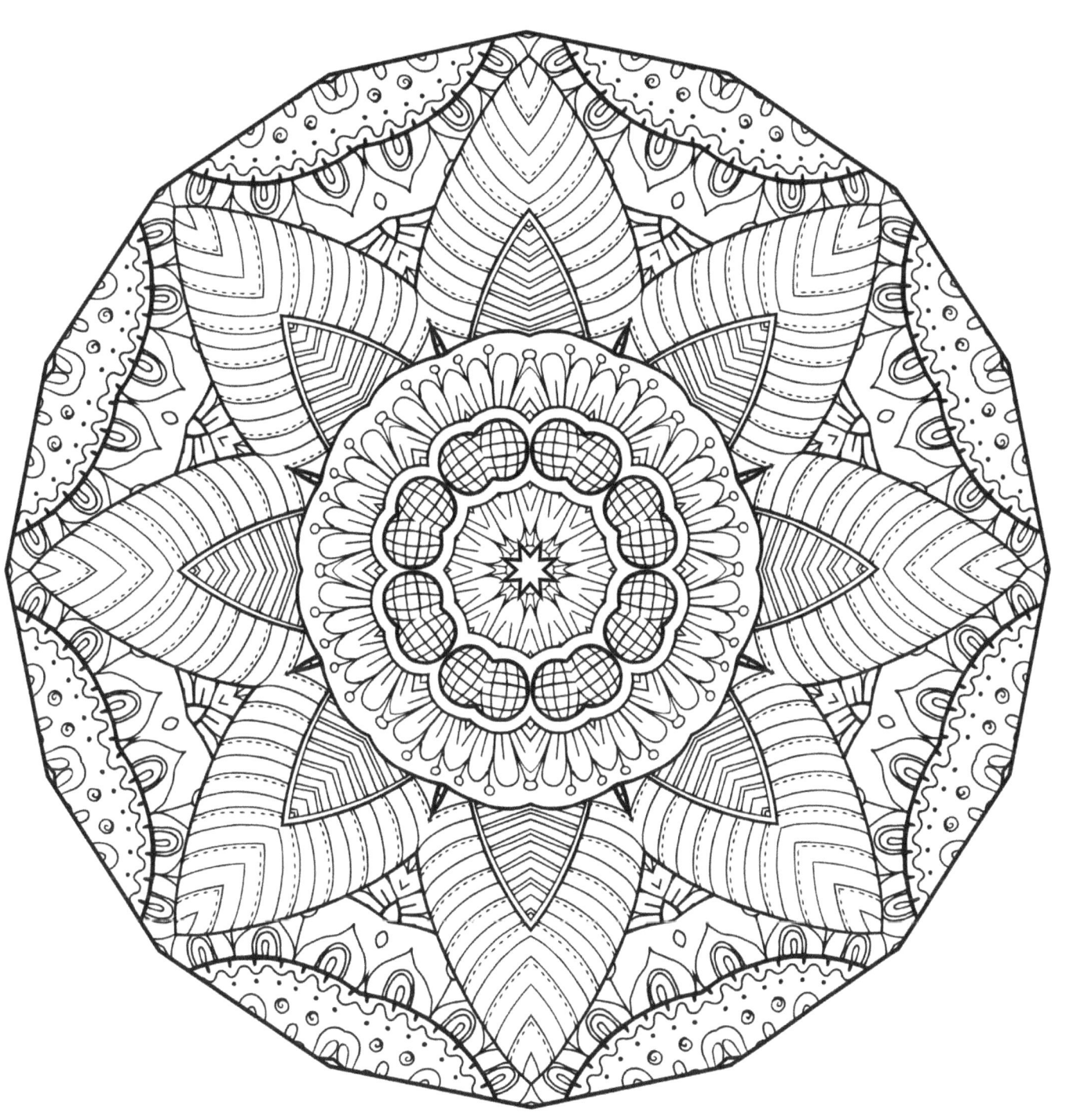

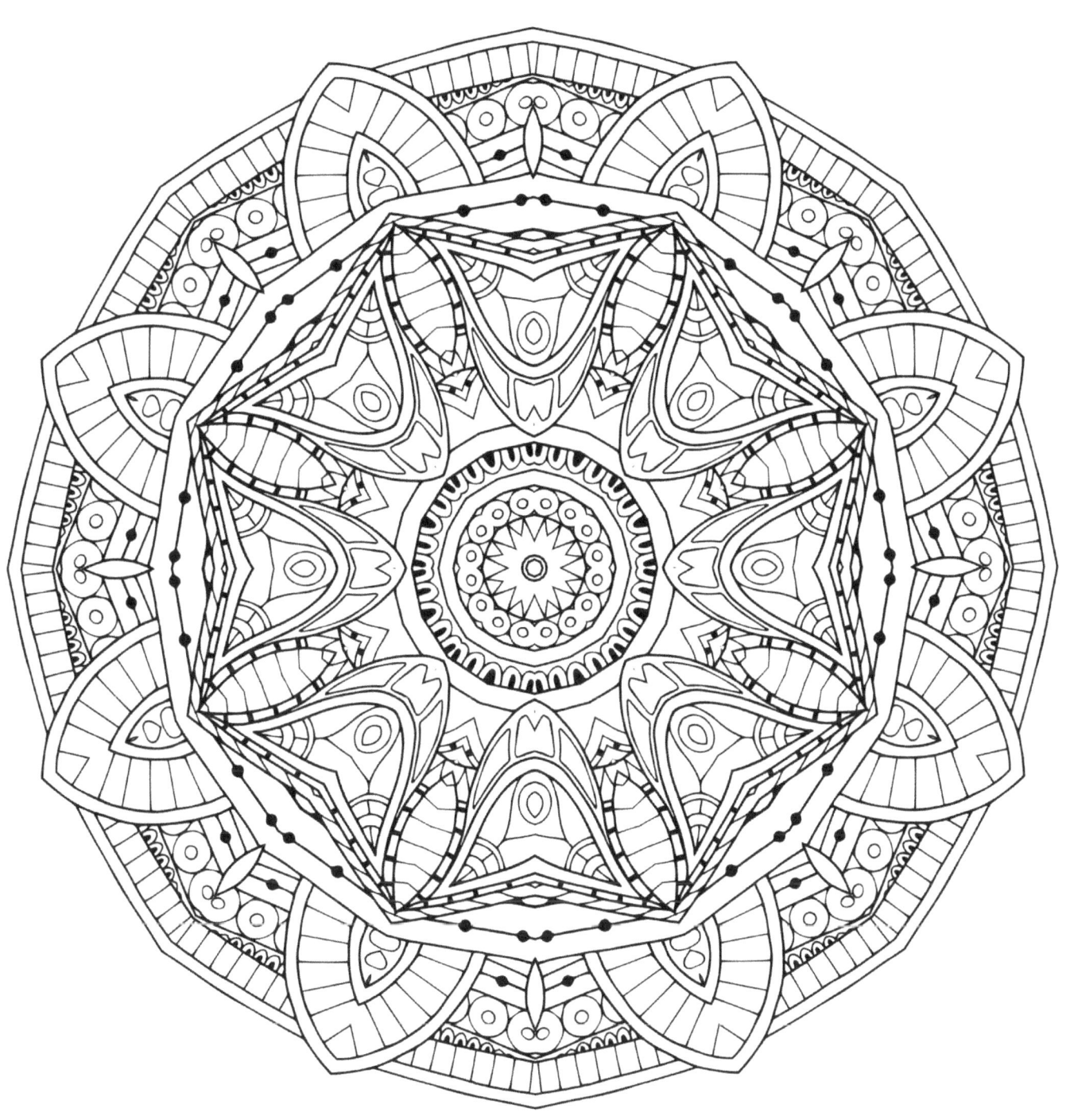

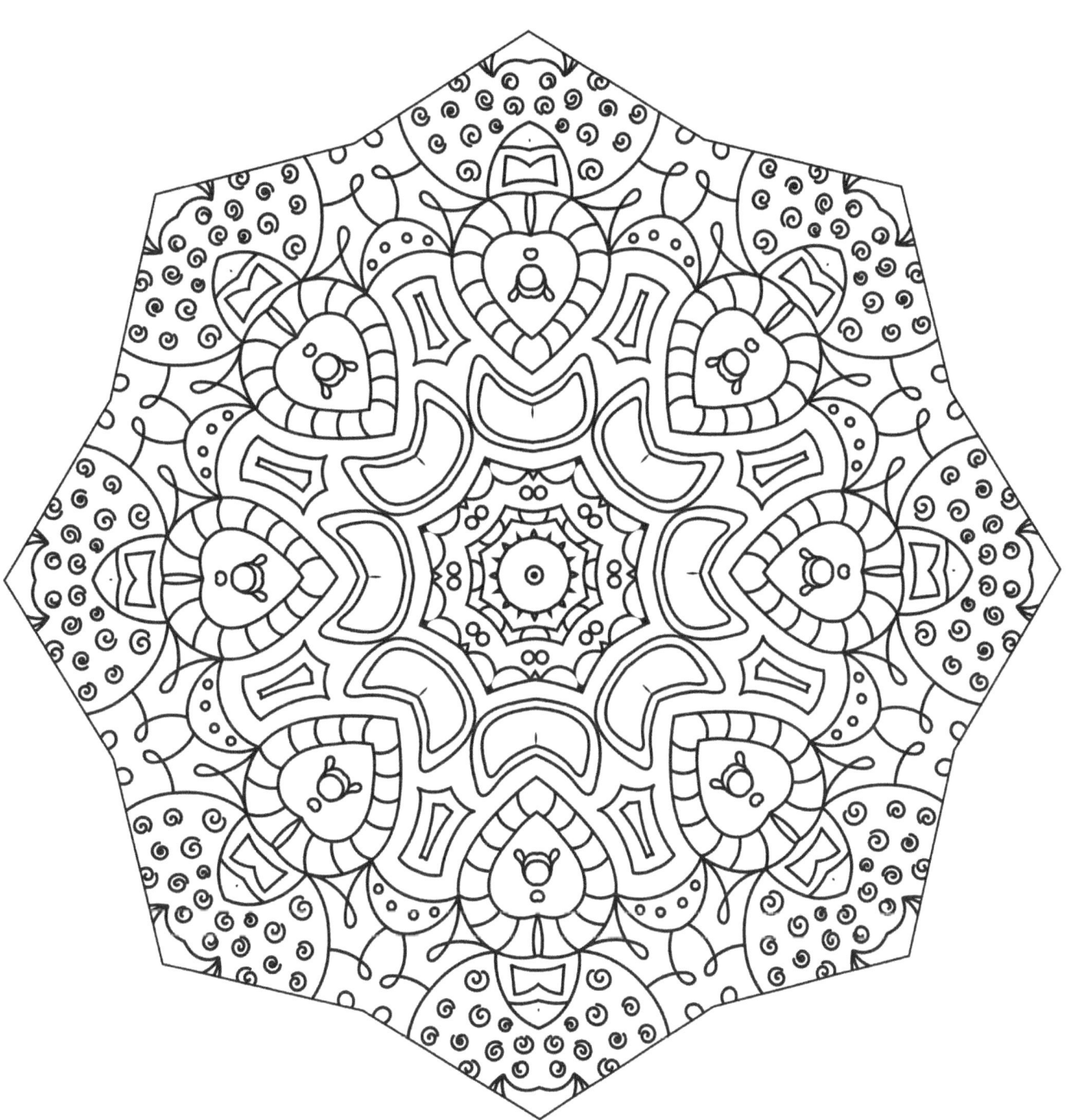

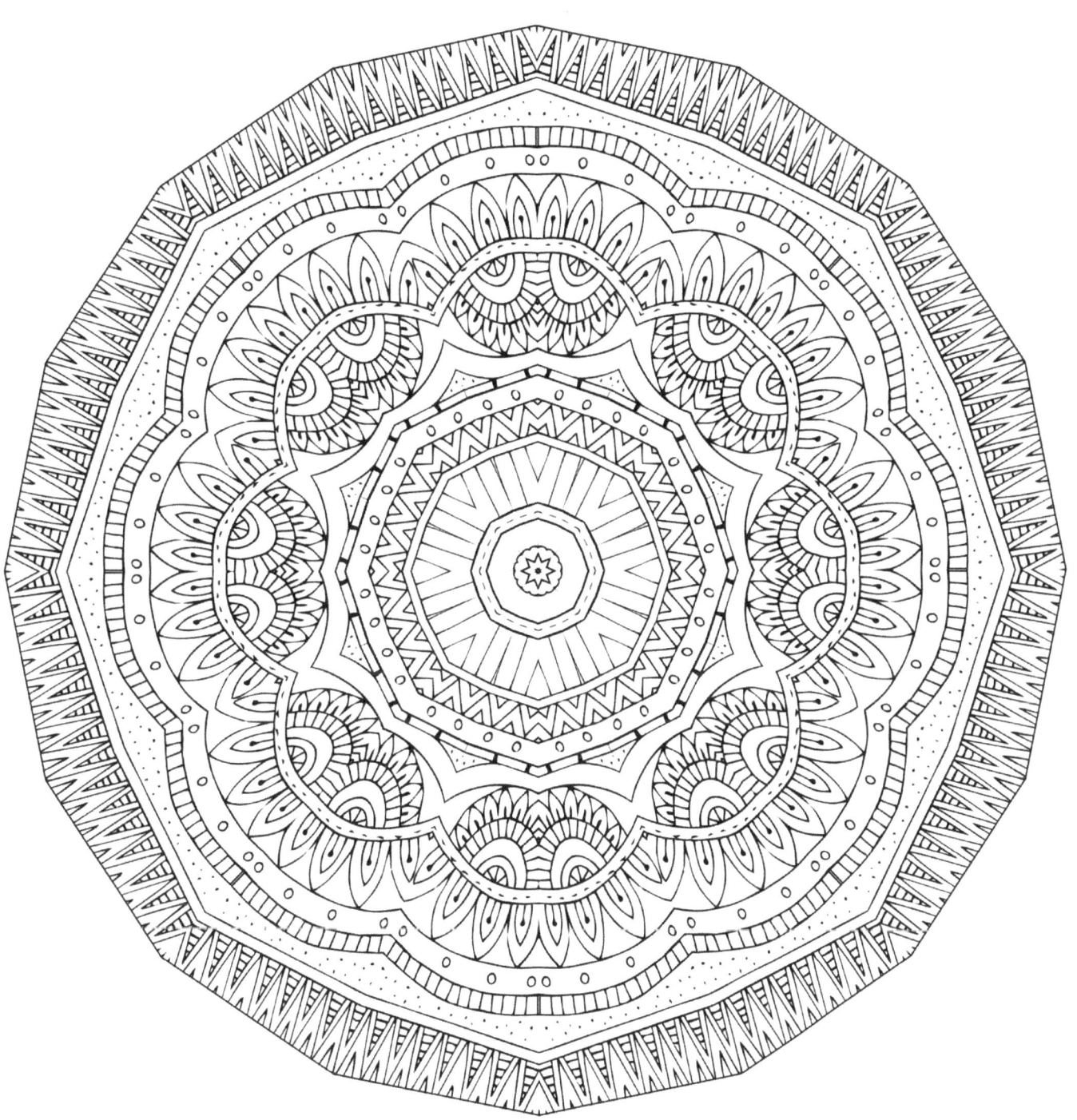

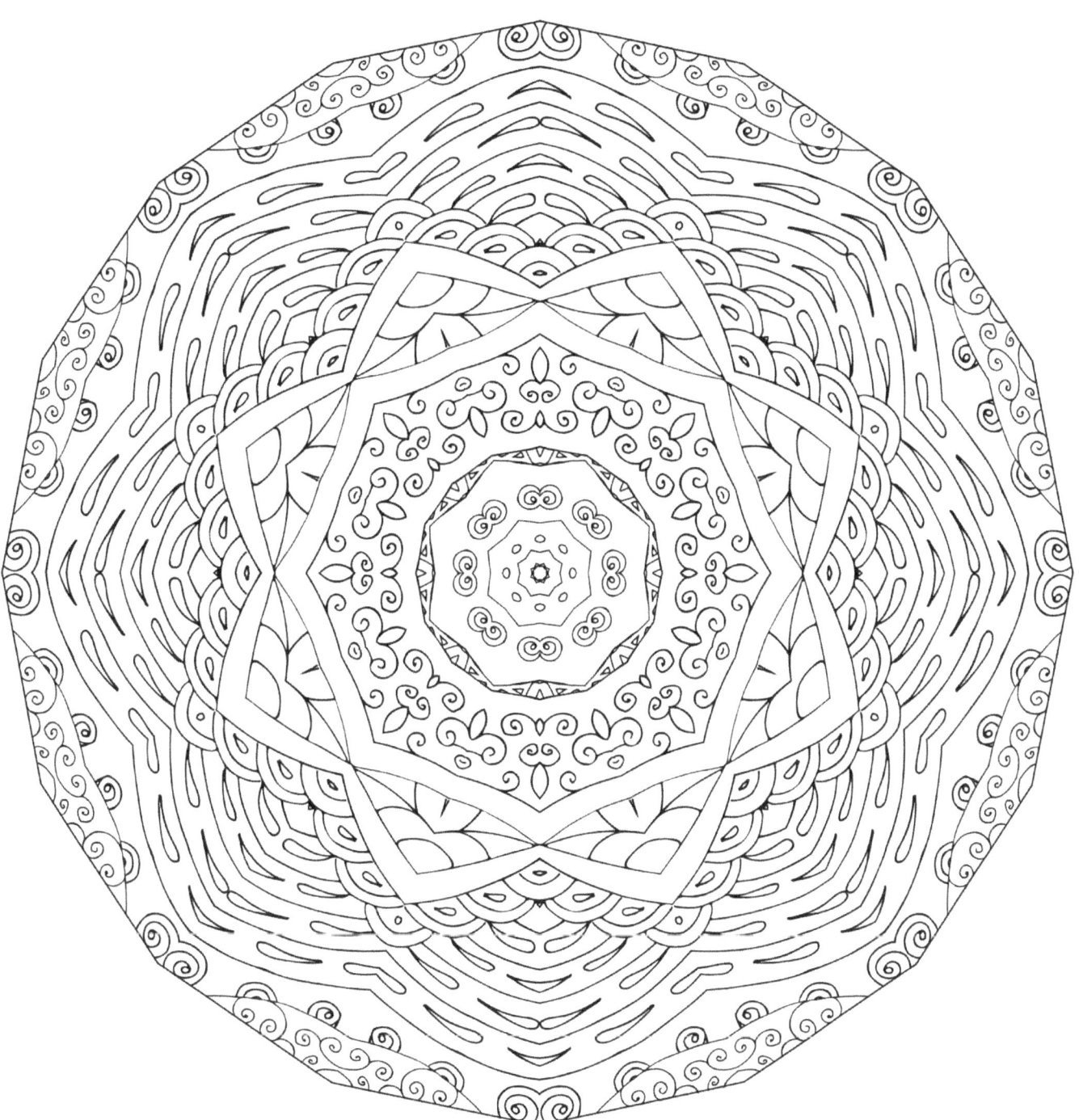

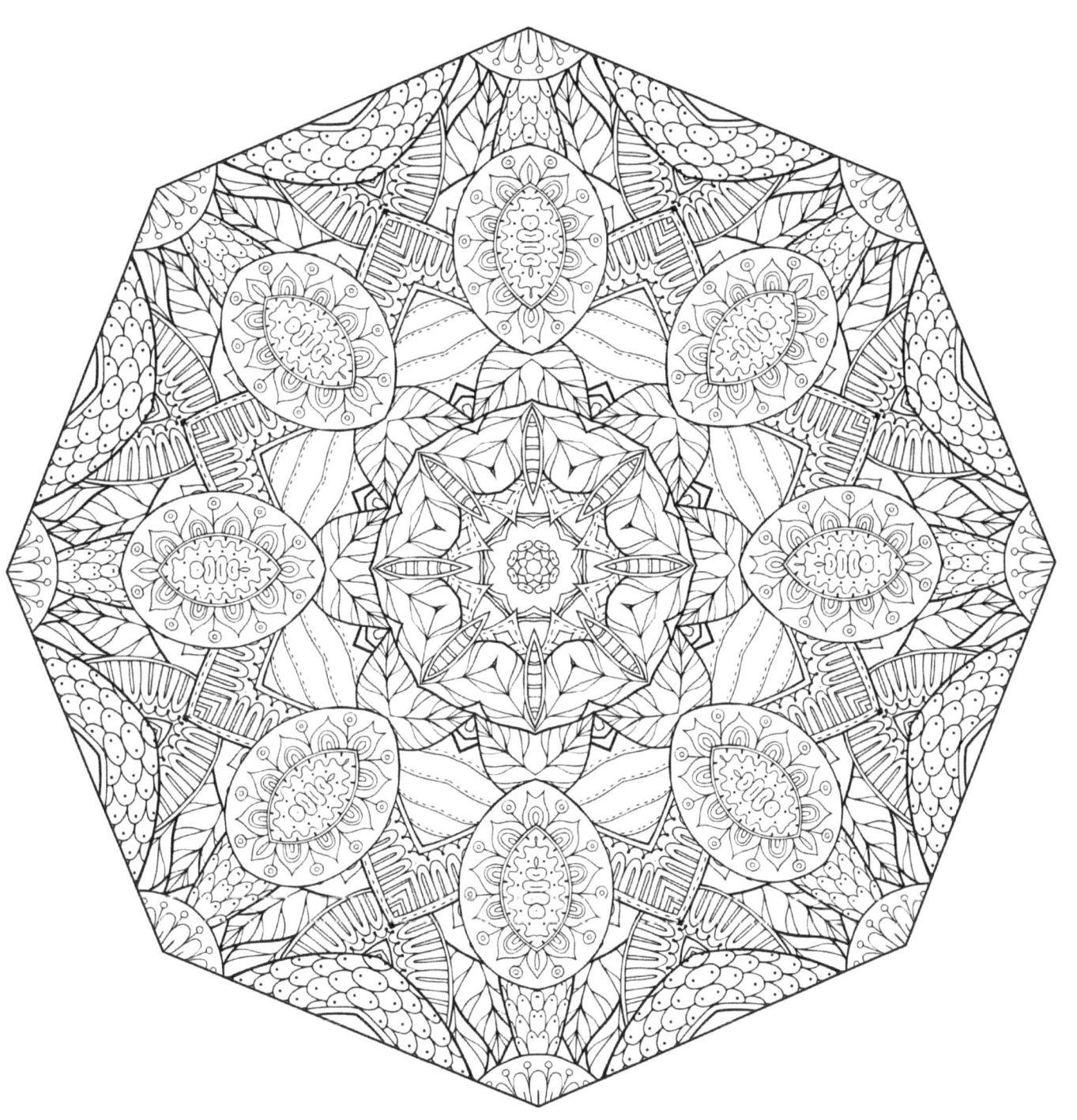

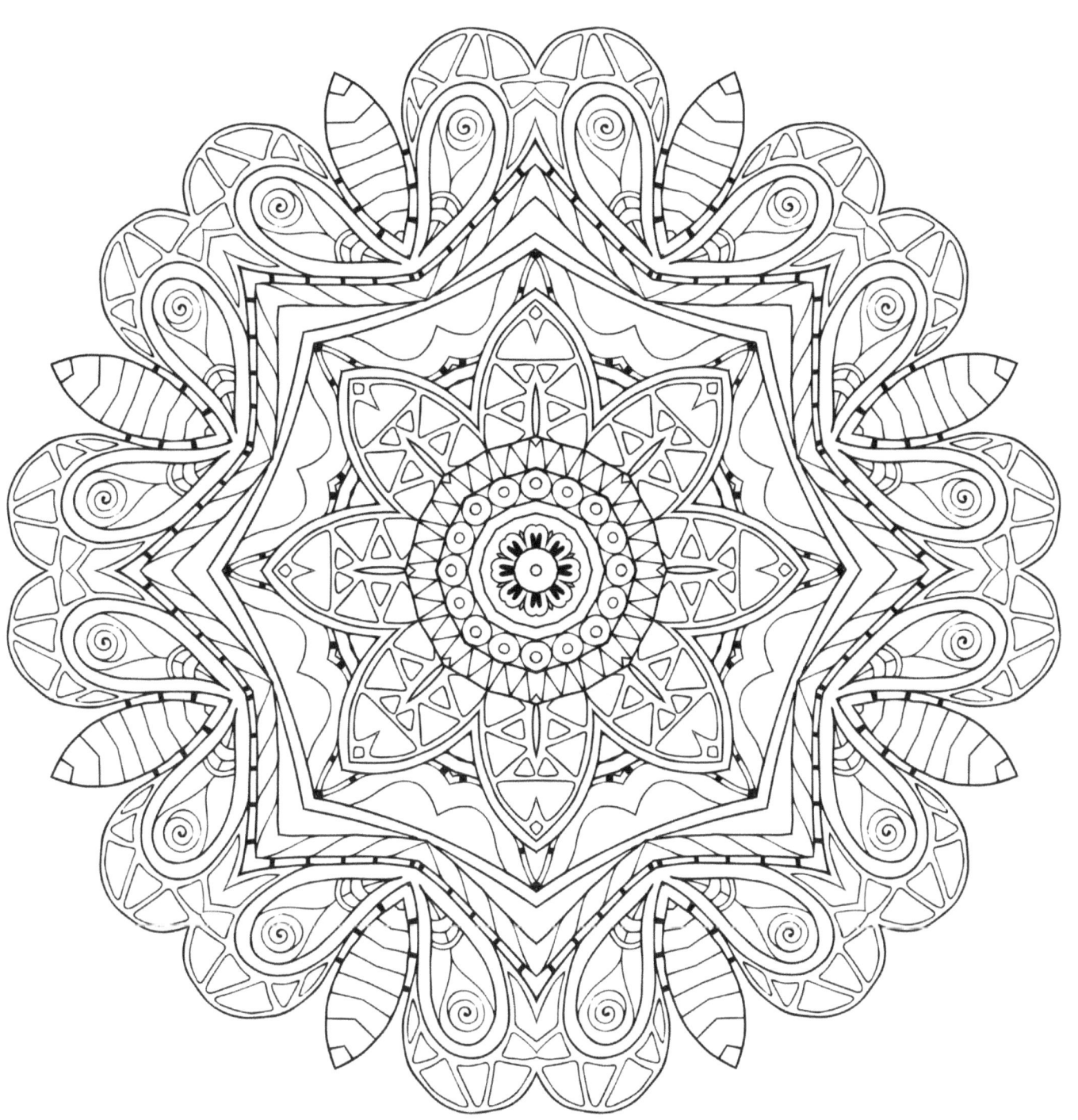

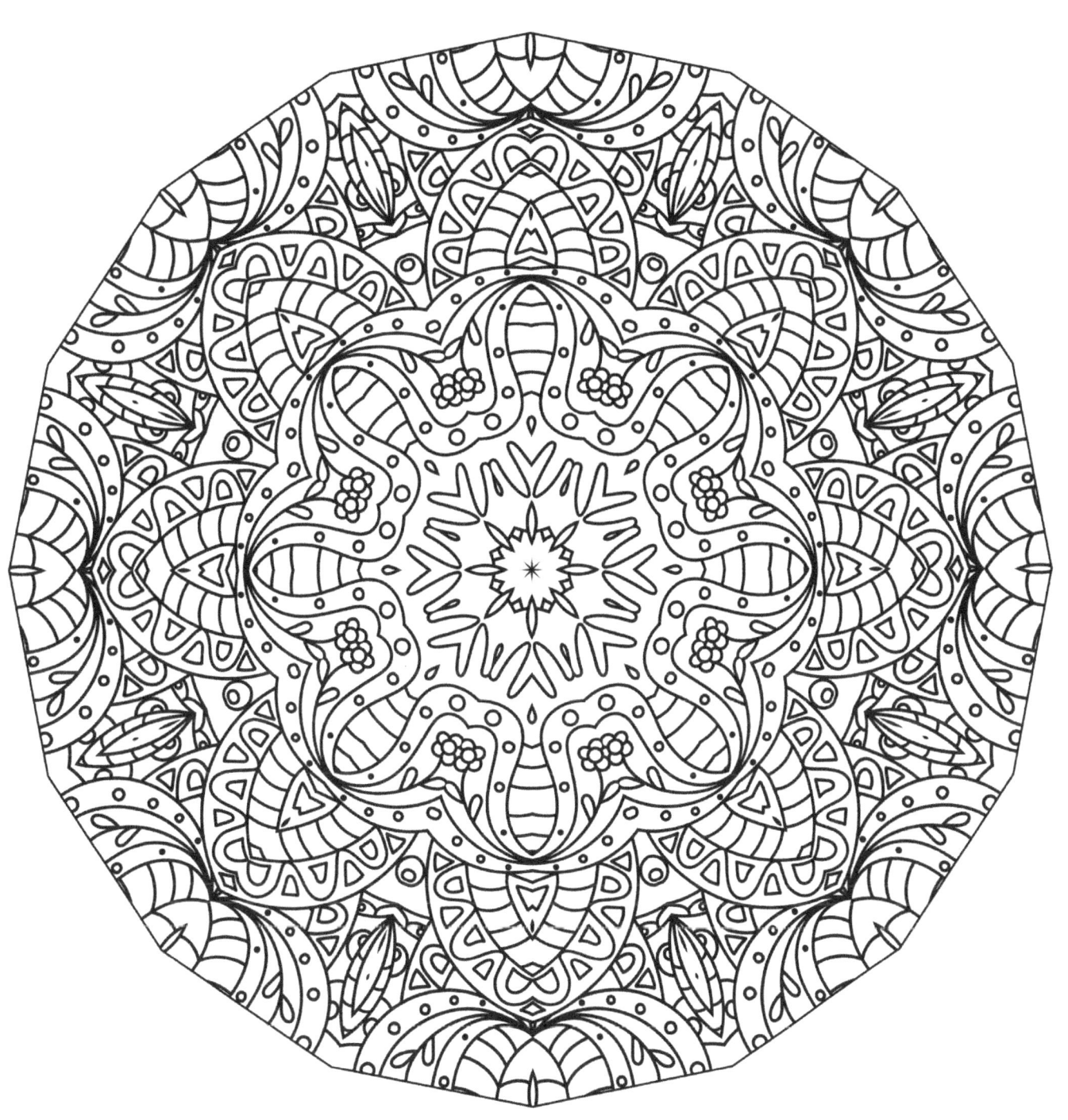

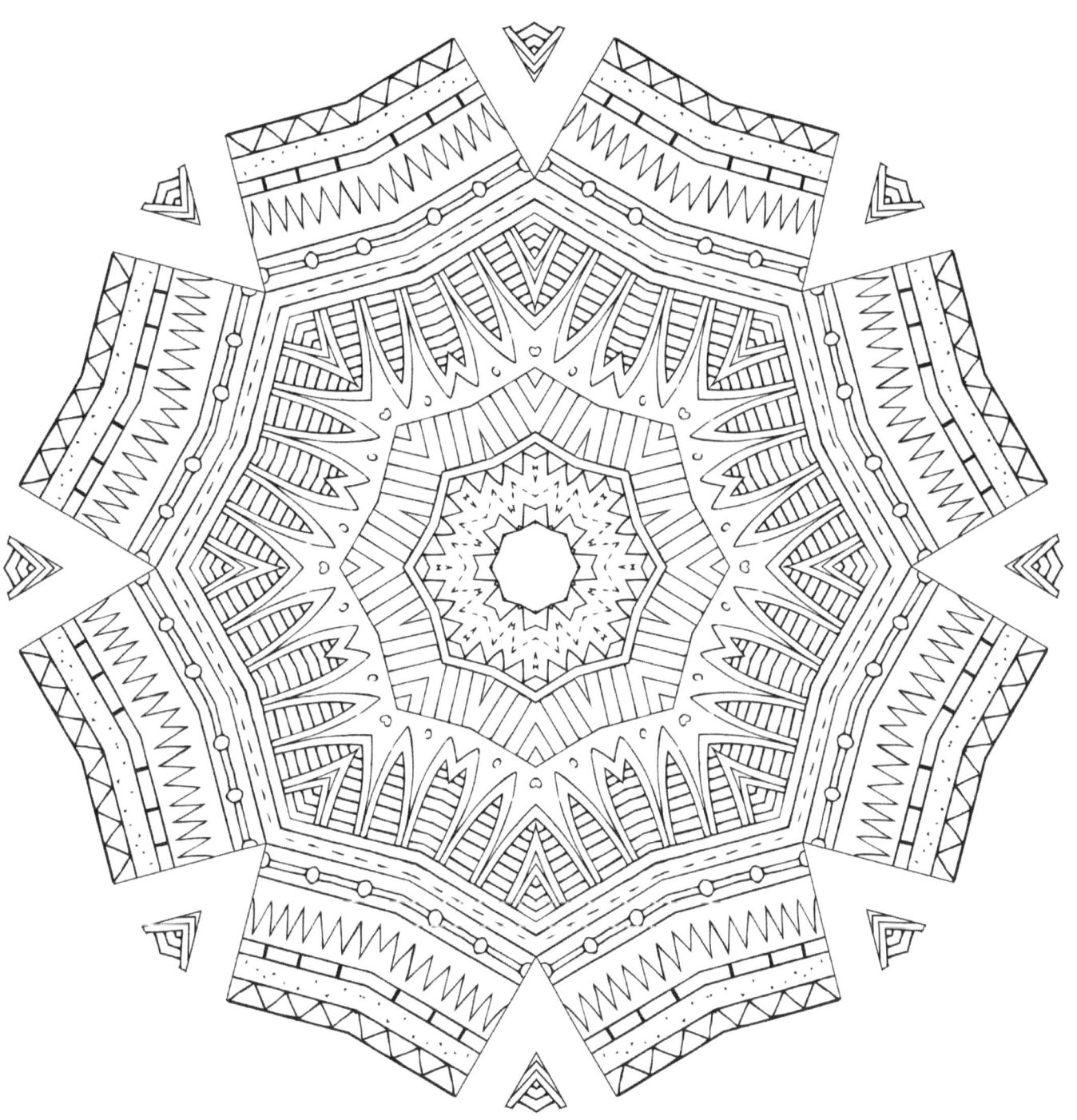

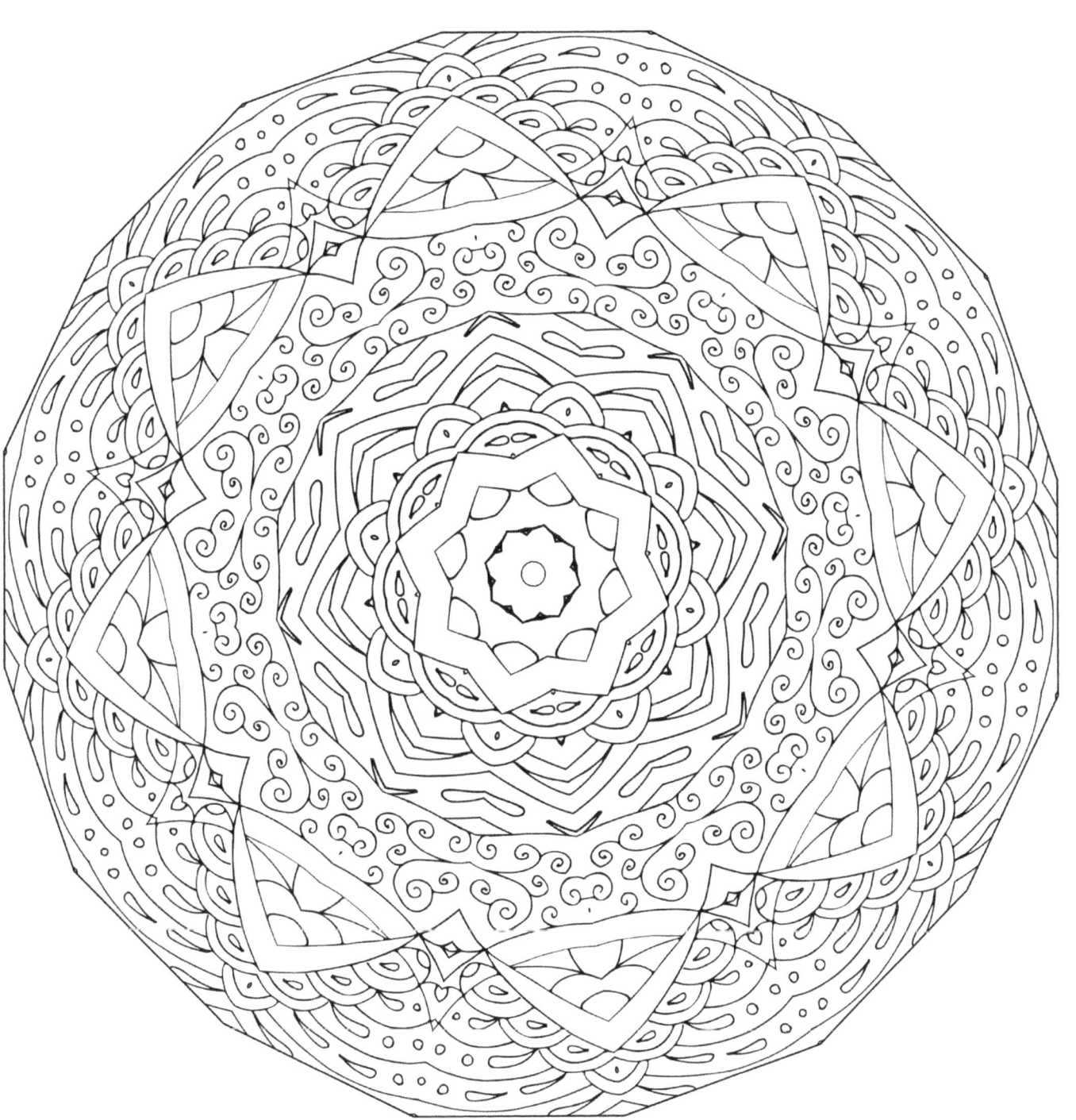

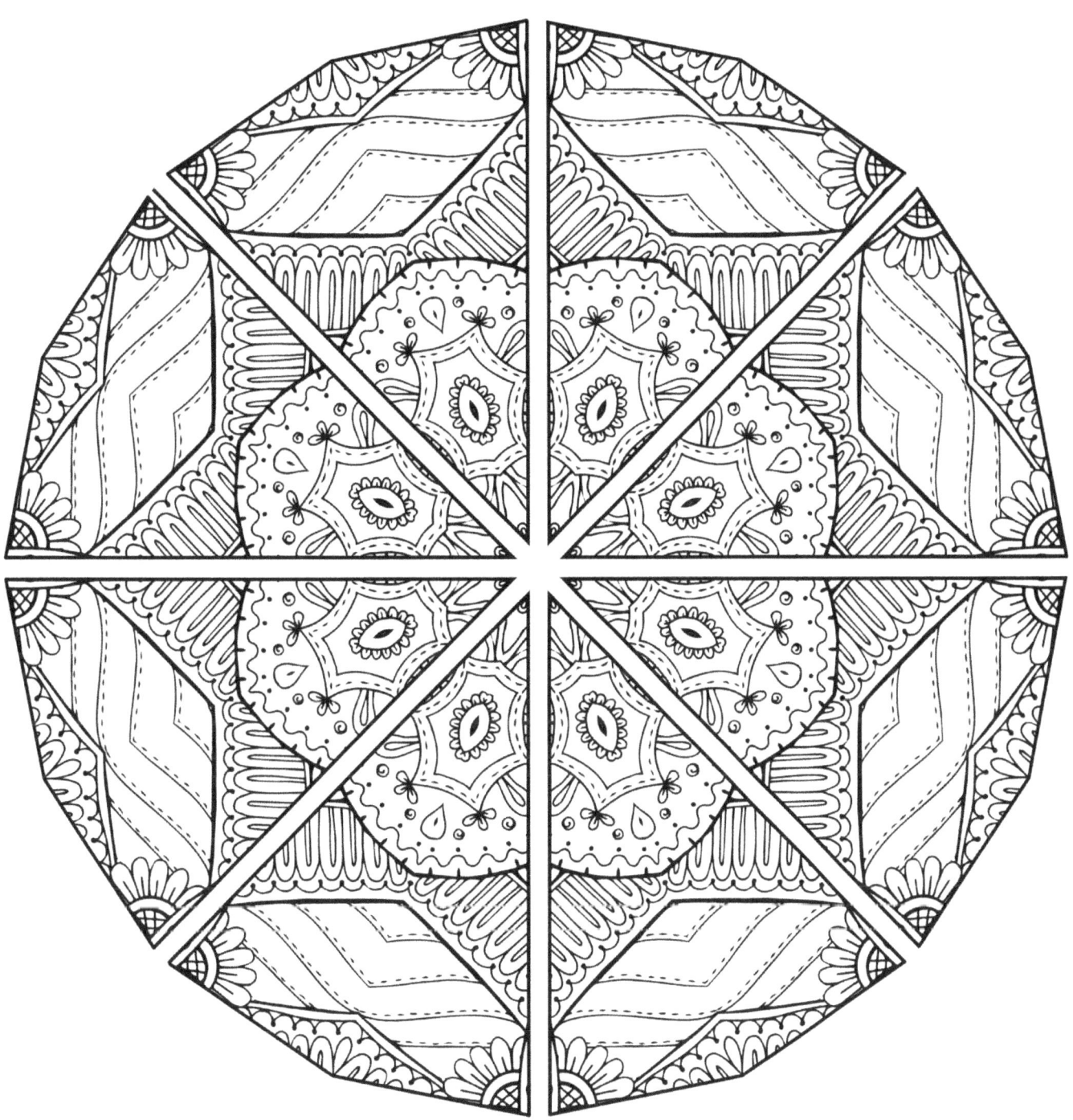

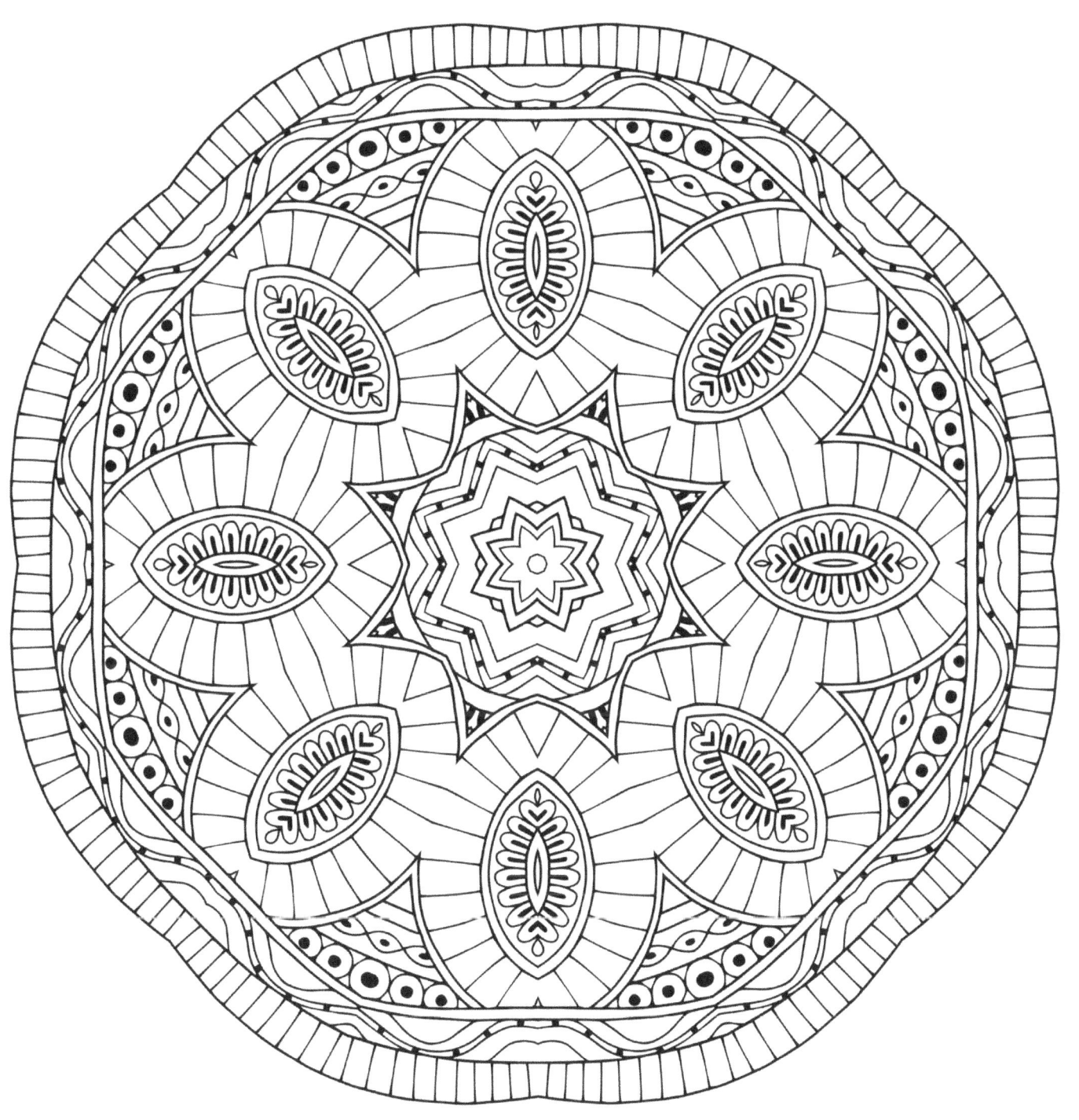

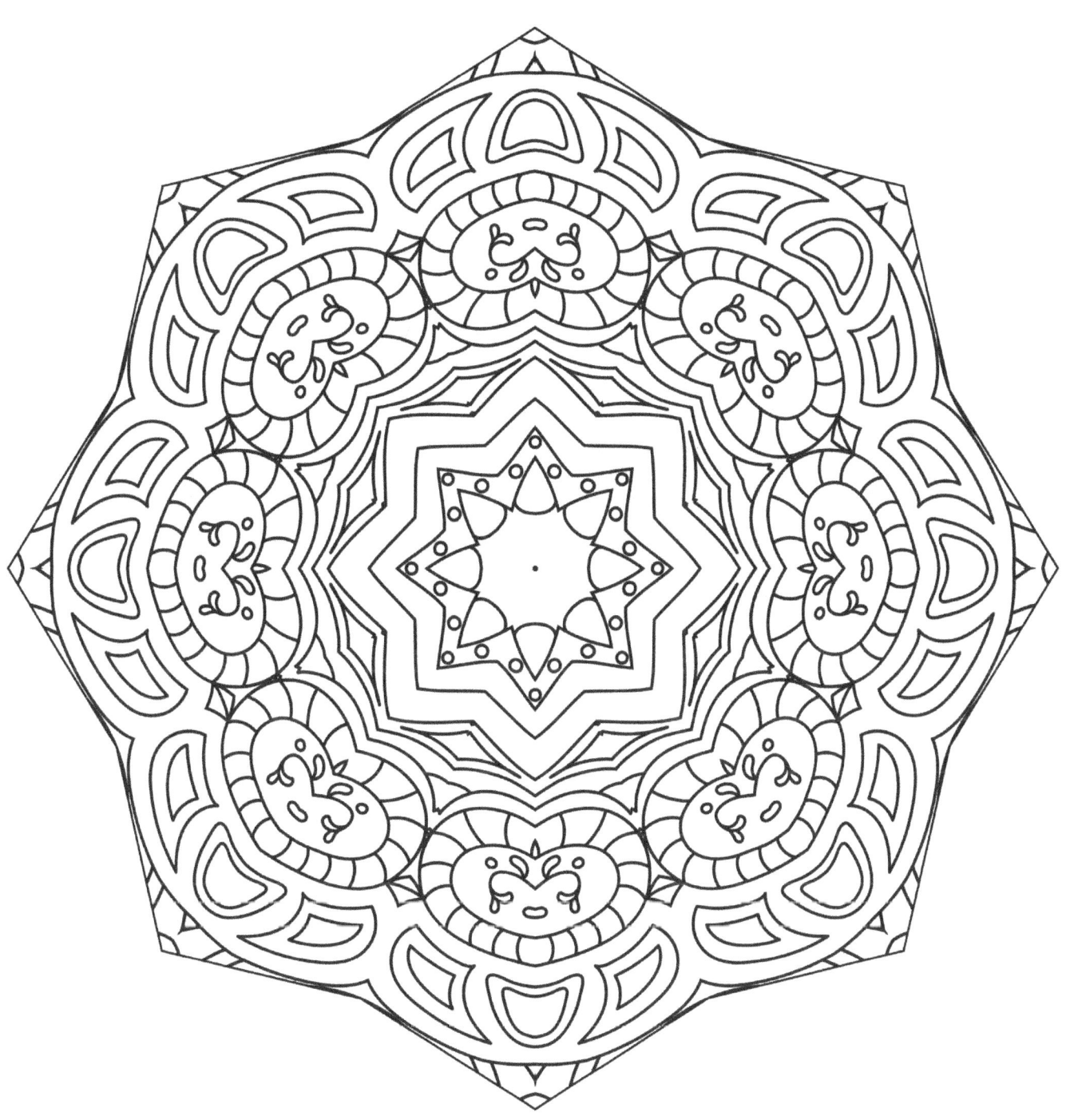

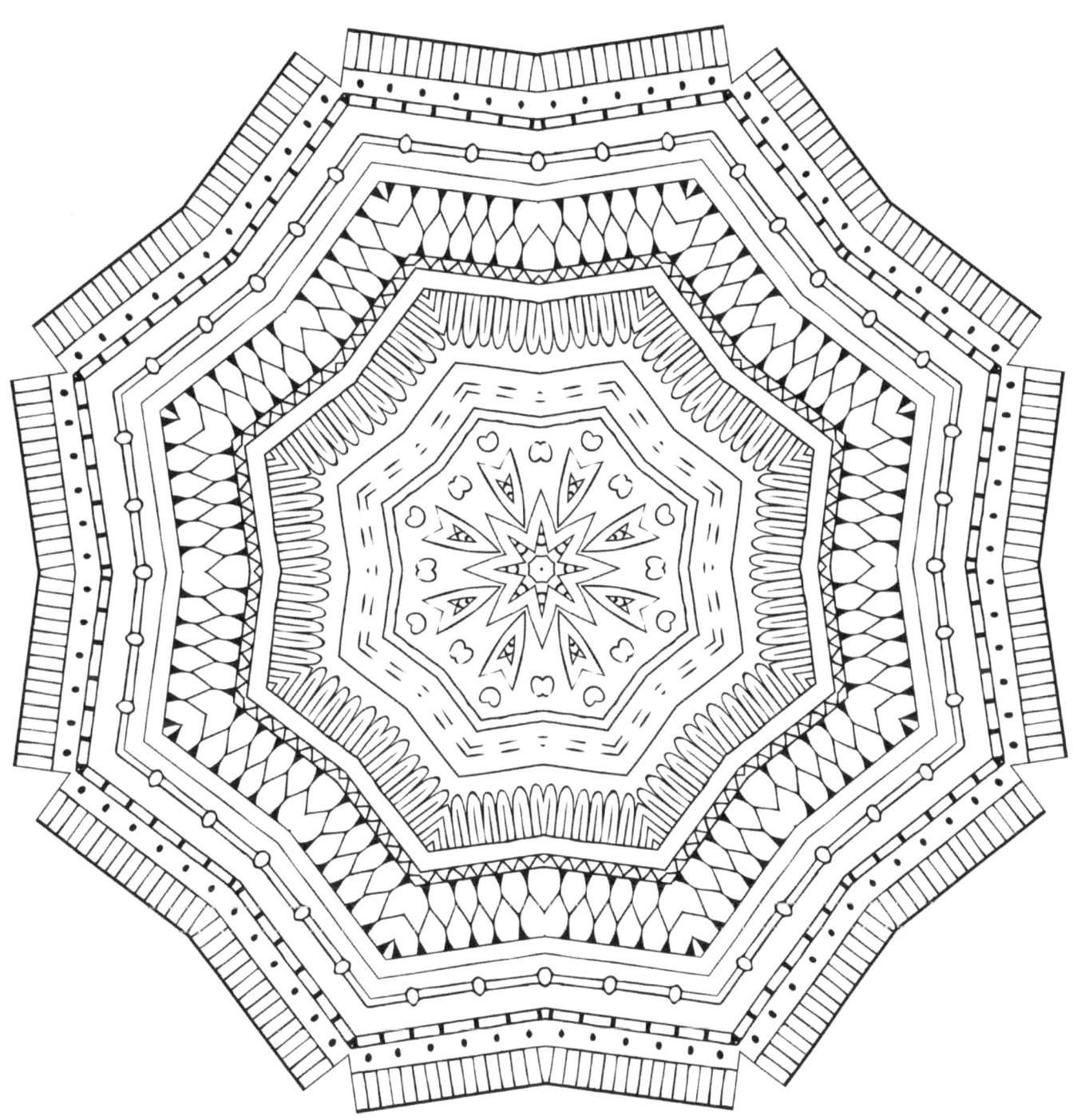

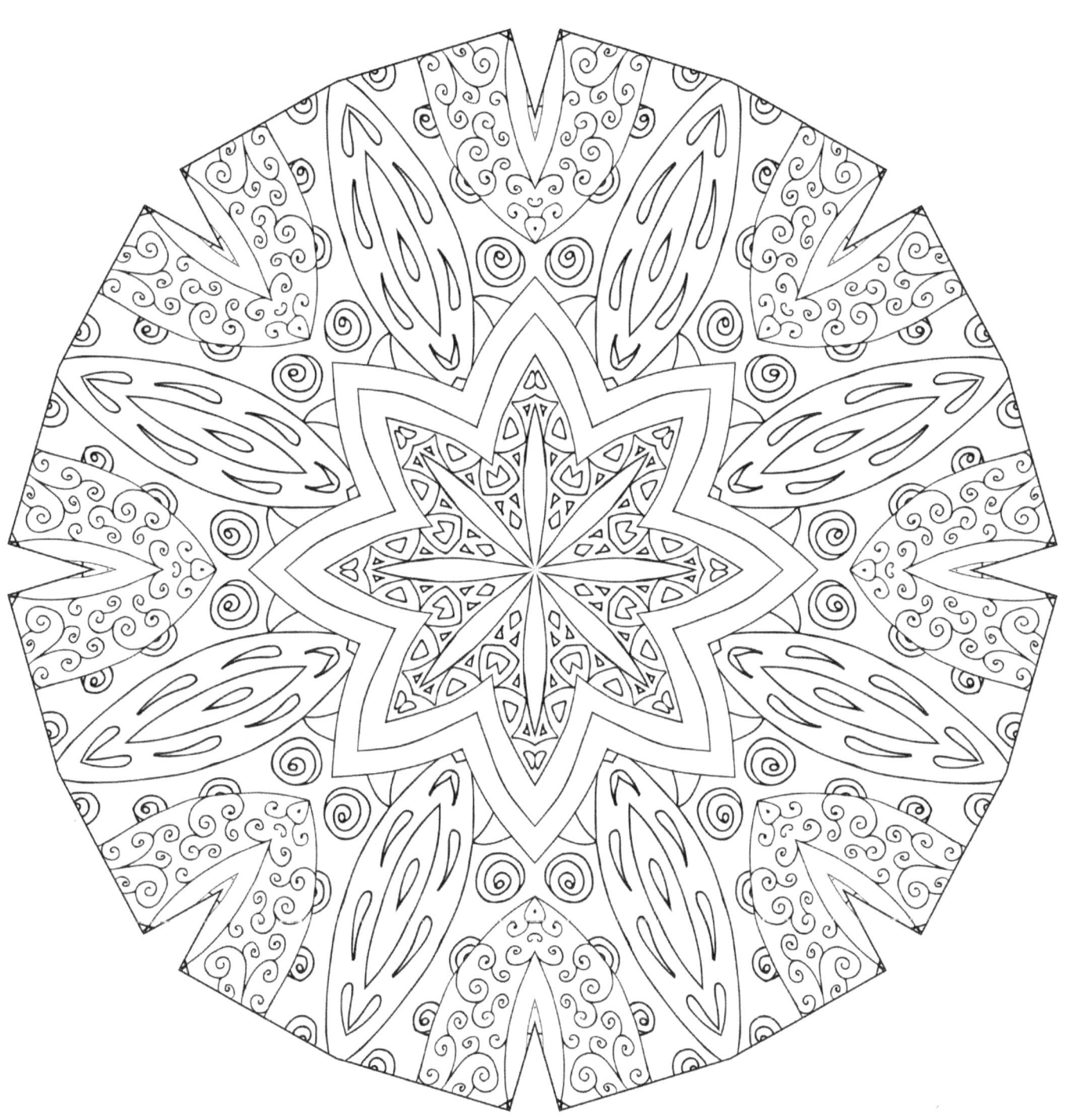

Coloring Companions Resources

Visit my website for a list of suggested resources to increase your coloring enjoyment!

KipADoodles.com/resources

Have coloring accessories that you love? Let me know about them at Kip@KipADoodles.com and I'll add them to the Resources list on my website!

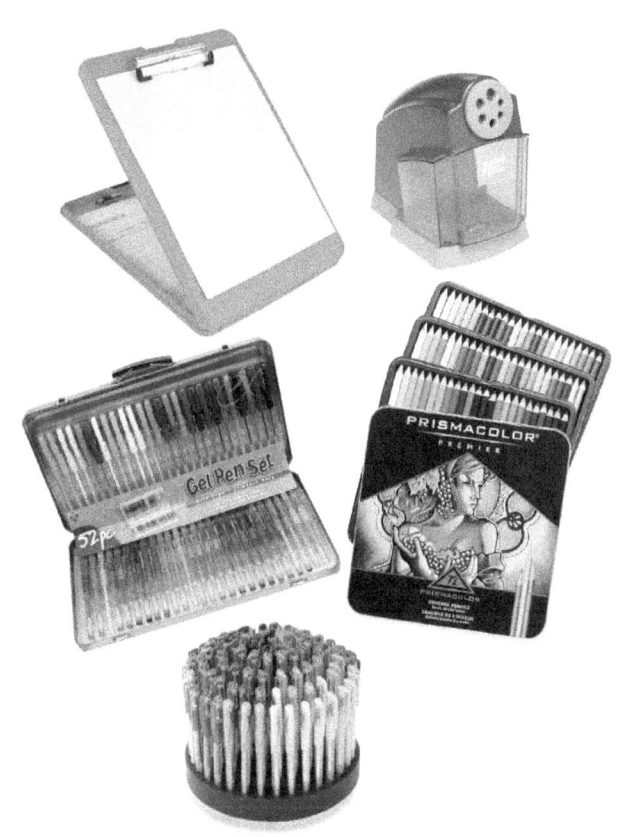

Other Recommended Coloring Books

REMEMBER: For Kip aDoodles News, Latest Coloring Books, and Special Discounts, **SUBSCRIBE HERE** >> **http://kipadoodles.com/subscribe**

Visit my website for a list of other recommended coloring books to increase your coloring enjoyment!

KipADoodles.com/recommended-books

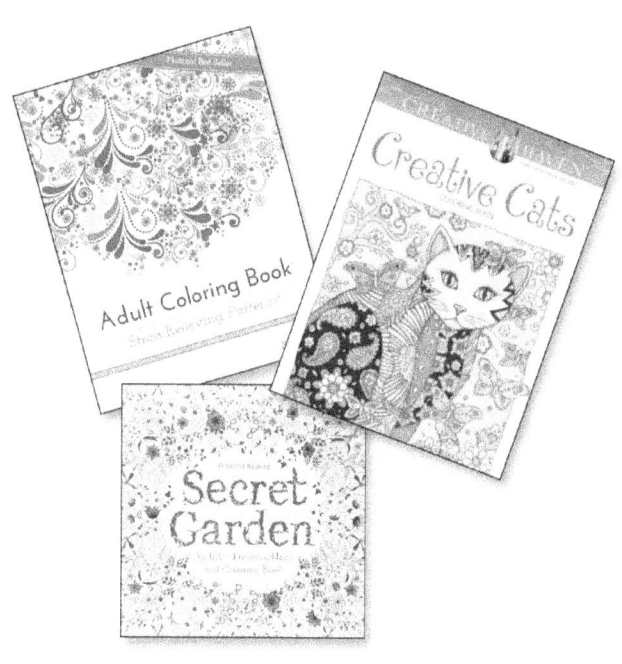

Now a Request From The Author

Did you enjoy this book?

If so, I have a small favor (that would mean a lot to me) to ask...

Would you take just a minute to leave an honest review? (Pretty please with a cherry on top!)

Just a sentence or two that tells people what you liked about this coloring book. Your words and stars will go a long way towards letting other colorists know they'll like this coloring book, too!

Did I mention pretty please with a cherry on top?

Here's the direct link:

http://kipadoodles.com/MandsVol1

Thank you & Happy coloring!

About The Author

Kip has been drawing, coloring and doodling since she could hold a pencil. Or more likely a crayon...Ha ha! Since then she has found many outlets for her design creativity, including as a web designer since 1993 (Yes, 1993!).

She has worked in just about every media - from embroidery to crewel to sewing to cross stitch to needlepoint to painting to drawing to jewelry design to counted cross stitch design... and more!

Bright colors, clean - and fun - designs are her passion! She also loves when the completed item is visually interesting, joyful and beautiful.

In her drawing for adult coloring books, she tries to create entertaining, intricate patterns and designs that spur the imagination and inspire the heart – as drawing inspires hers.

Kip lives on the road – and has since May 2013. She loves the fun adventure, great experiences, new friends, and endless inspiration!

www.ingramcontent.com/pod-product-compliance
Lightning Source LLC
Chambersburg PA
CBHW081628220526
45468CB00009B/2344